Natural History Museum
Dinosaur sticker book

Contents

Use the stickers on page 17 to fill in the missing dinosaurs.

What is a dinosaur?

Dinosaurs are a group of reptiles that roamed the Earth for over 140 million years.

Some could glide between trees, such as *Microraptor* (*MIKE-row-rap-tor*) and *Archaeopteryx* (*ark-ee-OPT-er-ix*).

Some dinosaurs walked on two legs, and some on four. Some were very fast, and some were slower.

Dinosaurs such as *Brachiosaurus* (*BRAK-ee-oh-sore-us*) were vegetarians. We call these herbivores.

Others such as *Deinonychus* (*die-non-ick-us*) were meat-eaters. We call these carnivores.

We can group dinosaurs together by looking at their different physical features. Their horns, feet or scales of armour can be used to identify different types of dinosaur.

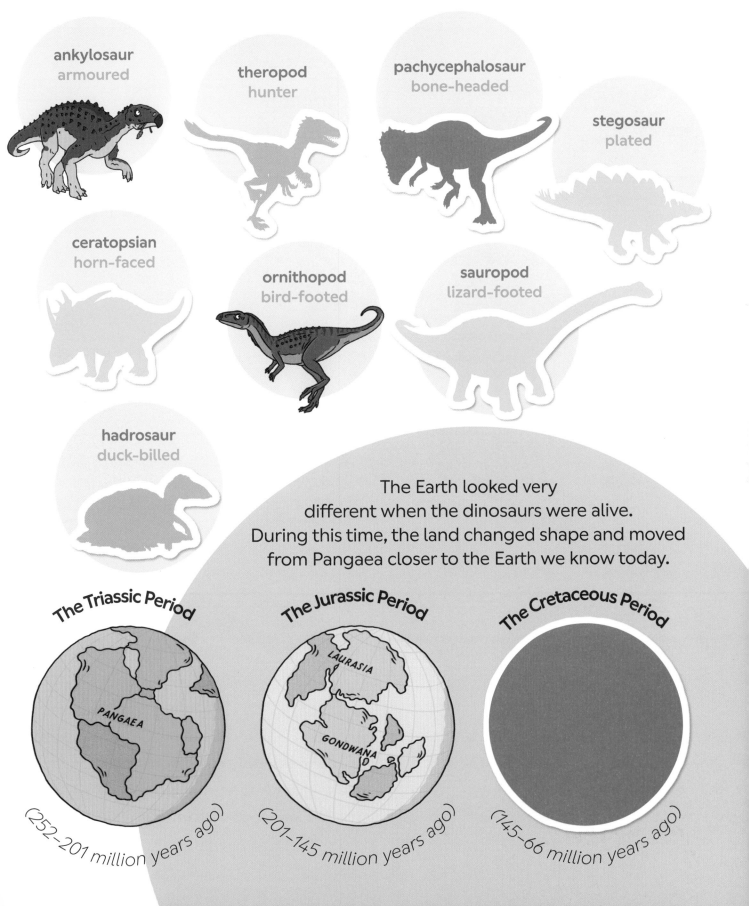

ankylosaur
armoured

theropod
hunter

pachycephalosaur
bone-headed

stegosaur
plated

ceratopsian
horn-faced

ornithopod
bird-footed

sauropod
lizard-footed

hadrosaur
duck-billed

The Earth looked very different when the dinosaurs were alive. During this time, the land changed shape and moved from Pangaea closer to the Earth we know today.

The Triassic Period

PANGAEA

(252–201 million years ago)

The Jurassic Period

LAURASIA

GONDWANA

(201–145 million years ago)

The Cretaceous Period

(145–66 million years ago)

The hunters

Most hunters were a type of dinosaur called theropods. They walked on two legs and were meat-eaters, with sharp, serrated teeth and curved claws.

These hunters could be very small such as *Microraptor* (MIKE-row-rap-tor), or they could be terrifyingly large, such as *Tyrannosaurus rex* (tie-RAN-oh-sore-us rex). Let's explore some of the larger members of the group.

Microraptor

Giganotosaurus
(gig-an-OH-toe-SORE-us)
Gigantosaurus looked like *Tyrannosaurus* but it was slimmer and taller and had three fingers, not two.

T. rex

Irritator
(irr-it-ate-or)
When scientists first studied this dinosaur's skull, the bones were tricky to rearrange, so they decided to name it *Irritator*.

Use the stickers on pages 17–18 to fill in the missing dinosaurs.

Allosaurus
(AL-oh-saw-russ)
Allosaurus was a fierce hunter with enormous, curved teeth. It could take down a *Stegosaurus!*

Baryonyx
(bah-ree-ON-icks)
Baryonyx had a crocodile-shaped mouth. It also had a large claw on its hand which it used to hook fish out of the water.

Megalosaurus
(MEG-ah-low-sore-us)
One of the first dinosaurs ever discovered in the world, *Megalosaurus* was found in England.

Spinosaurus
(SPY-noh-sore-us)
The longest meat-eater had a big sail along its back. It was the same length as one and a half London buses.

Albertosaurus
(al-BERT-oh-saw-russ)
This saw-toothed hunter was related to *Tyrannosaurus*, and was a deadly and dangerous predator.

The most famous small theropod was probably the ferocious *Velociraptor* (vel-OSS-ee-rap-tor), **which could sprint faster than an African elephant can today, but there are plenty more to explore.**

Chirostenotes
(kie-ro-sten-oh-teez)
Chirostenotes had long fingers and claws that it used to forage for insects.

Microraptor
(MIKE-row-rap-tor)
Microraptor was a tiny, feathered dinosaur with sharp, pointed teeth.

Scipionyx
(sip-ee-OH-nicks)
This tiny dinosaur was only 20 cm (8 in) long.

Bambiraptor
(bam-bee-rap-tor)
Bambiraptor had extremely sharp claws. It was first discovered in North America.

Oviraptor
(OH-vee-RAP-tor)
Originally known as the 'egg thief', scientists now think that *Oviraptor* sat on its nest like birds do today.

Use the stickers on page 18 to complete the scene.

Confuciusornis
(konn-few-shus-or-niss)
Found in China, *Confuciusornis* had a beak but no teeth. It was an early form of bird dinosaur.

Archaeopteryx
(ark-ee-OPT-er-ix)
Even though its name means 'ancient wing', *Archaeopteryx* wasn't very good at flying.

Caudipteryx (caw-dip-ter-iks)
This birdlike hunter may have swallowed stones to help digest the food in its stomach.

Compsognathus
(komp-sog-NATH-us)
'Compys' were chickensized and used their speed and quick reactions to hunt.

Troodon
(TROH-oh-don)
Troodon, like all dinosaurs, laid its eggs in a nest, probably made of mud, on the ground.

Coelophysis
(seel-OH-fie-sis)
Like other meat-eating dinosaurs, *Coelophysis* didn't weigh much because it had hollow bones like birds today.

The giants

Use the stickers on page 19 to fill in the missing dinosaurs.

Sauropods were the giants of the dinosaur world. They were herbivores and walked on four legs. They had long necks and tails, but small heads.

Nigersaurus
(nee-zhayr-sore-us)
Nigersaurus had 100 teeth that it used to chop up plants before sucking them up like a prehistoric vacuum cleaner.

Alamosaurus
(ah-la-mow-SORE-us)
Fossils of this sauropod measuring the same as two London buses have been dug up in North America.

Apatosaurus
(ah-PAT-oh-sore-us)
Apatosaurus had an enormous stomach that it used to ferment – or rot – its food for up to two weeks.

Brachiosaurus
(BRAK-ee-oh-sore-us)
This giant's front legs were longer than its back legs, which meant it could eat the highest leaves in the trees.

Diplodocus
(DIP-low-DOCK-us)
Spot its long neck that could reach up high and down low for food and water. It could wave its tail around like a powerful whip.

Anchisaurus (ANK-ee-sore-us) and *Plateosaurus (plat-ee-oh-sore-us)* were some of the first herbivores. They were smaller, with shorter necks, and probably walked on two legs.

Vulcanodon
(vul-kan-oh-don)
This dinosaur's name means 'volcano tooth'. It was given the name because its fossil was found between two layers of volcanic lava.

Cetiosaurus
(see-TEE-oh-sore-us)
Its name means 'whale-lizard' because its remains were found in marine rocks.

Shunosaurus
(SHOON-oh-SORE-us)
Can you see its club-like tail which it used to fight off attackers?

Amargasaurus (A-MARG-oh-sore-us)
Look at the magnificent rows of spines on the neck and back of this giant. Scientists think that they held up two sails of skin for display or signalling.

Plates and spines

Some plant-eating dinosaurs developed armour plates and spines to protect themselves from predators. They could also fight back with their clubbed or spiky tails.

Use the stickers on page 20 to fill in the missing dinosaurs.

Huayangosaurus
(hoy-YANG-oh-SORE-us)
Can you spot the spines on its shoulders? Scientists aren't sure if these were for defending themselves from predators or for display.

Nodosaurus
(no-doh-SORE-us)
Nodosaurus didn't fight back. It crouched down and used its rounded armour plates for protection instead.

Stegosaurus
(STEG-oh-SORE-us)
Stegosaurus had a powerful spiked tail. Its bony plates would warn off hunters and could possibly control its temperature.

Ankylosaurus *(an-KIE-loh-sore-us)*
One of the largest armoured dinosaurs, *Ankylosaurus* even had armour on its eyelids.

Sauropelta
(sore-oh-pelt-ah)
Heavy shoulder spines, which protected its neck, meant that *Sauropelta* couldn't move very quickly.

Euoplocephalus *(you-OH-plo-kef-ah-lus)*
It had a wide, flat head covered in armour to protect it from attack. Despite being big, this dinosaur had a very small brain.

Edmontonia
(ed-mon-TONE-ee-ah)
Similar to a crocodile's scales, this dinosaur's spiky armour had a bony core for extra strength and shielding.

Scelidosaurus
(skel-EYE-doh-sore-us)
Look at its bony armour! This dinosaur was only 4 m (12 ft) long.

Use the stickers on pages 20-21 to fill in the missing dinosaurs.

Bone heads and horns

Some plant-eating dinosaurs developed fierce horns as well as bony neck frills. And some had parrot-like beaks which they used to tear through plants.

Triceratops
(tri-SERRA-tops)
With its horns, beak and huge neck frill, *Triceratops* is one of the strangest-looking dinosaurs to ever exist.

Protoceratops
(pro-toe-ser-ah-tops)
One fossil of this small dinosaur shows it being attacked by a *Velociraptor*. They were buried by a sandstorm while they fought.

Styracosaurus (sty-RAK-oh-sore-us)
Spot the long spikes on the neck frill of *Styracosaurus*! It used them to protect itself, as it couldn't outrun its predators.

Centrosaurus
(cen-TROH-sore-us)
Look at the spines on its neck frill. This dinosaur lived in large groups that moved from one place to another.

Pachyrhinosaurus
(pack-ee-RINE-oh-sore-us)
Its name means 'thick-nosed lizard' as it didn't have a horn. Instead it had an area of flat rough bone on its head.

Pachycephalosaurus
(pack-ee-KEF-ah-loh-SORE-us)
This dome-headed dinosaur lived in the Late Cretaceous period.

Stegoceras
(ste-GOS-er-as)
Stegoceras was a bone-headed dinosaur that may have bumped heads with other rival dinosaurs.

The bone heads had thick, ridged skulls and belonged to the group called pachycephalosaurs. All of them ate only plants. We call these dinosaurs herbivores.

Duck bills and short beaks

This group of dinosaurs are called ornithopods. They were plant-eaters and had short beaks or duck-like bills which they used to tear through tough leaves.

Use the stickers on pages 21–22 to fill in the missing dinosaurs.

Tenontosaurus *(ten-ON-toe-sore-us)* *Tenontosaurus* was about the same size as a donkey, but its tail made up more than half of its length.

Edmontosaurus *(ed-MON-toe-sore-us)* This large ornithopod had 1,000 teeth which it used to grind conifer needles, twigs and seeds.

Hypsilophodon *(hip-sih-LOH-foh-don)* Scientists are puzzled by this dinosaur as they have only found young fossils, not any adult ones.

Camptosaurus *(KAMP-toe-sore-us)* Its name means 'bent dinosaur' and it is a relative of *Iguanodon*.

Lambeosaurus
(lam-BEE-oh-SORE-us)
Lambeosaurus had a bony crest on the top of its head which it used for signalling to other dinosaurs.

Iguanodon
(ig-WHA-noh-don)
Spot the large thumb spike on the end of its hand which it used to fight predators!

Maiasaura
(my-ah-SORE-ah)
Scientists think that *Maiasaura* nested in groups and cared for their young in large dinosaur nurseries.

Ouranosaurus
(oo-RAH-noh-sore-us)
Look at the long bones on the back of this dinosaur. They may have formed a sail used for display or to keep it cool.

Parasaurolophus
(pa-ra-saw-ROL-off-us)
This dinosaur's crest was hollow. When *Parasaurolophus* blew air through it, it made a loud noise that could be heard for miles.

The last days of the dinosaurs

Use the stickers on page 22 to fill in the missing dinosaurs.

Around 66 million years ago, life changed. A giant rock from space smashed into the Earth. This set off a chain reaction of earthquakes, volcanoes and huge tsunami waves. The impact itself threw dust into the air that blotted out the sun.

The destruction on Earth meant that many plants died, and so plant-eating dinosaurs, such as *Triceratops,* had no food left to eat.

As the herbivores perished, so did the hunters like *Tyrannosaurus* that preyed upon them.

After more than 140 million years, the reign of the dinosaurs was over. Most dinosaurs became extinct, but one small group, the theropods, evolved into birds and, with the other mammals, reptiles, insects and sealife that survived, adapted to the new conditions and continued to evolve into what lives on Earth today.